Rock & Roll Highway

The Robbie Robertson Story

SEBASTIAN ROBERTSON

illustrated by **ADAM GUSTAVSON**

Christy Ottaviano Books

HENRY HOLT AND COMPANY

NEW YORK

The Last Waltz

On Thanksgiving night in 1976 the crowd cheered wildly, stomping their feet, demanding the return of their favorite band. Having just completed a five-hour set of songs, The Band came out for one more. "You're still there?" Robbie spoke into the microphone, exciting the fans further. The Band then played their final song, their "Last Waltz."

After sixteen years of touring the world and sharing music with millions, Robbie Robertson put his guitar down, removed his hat, and stepped up to the microphone. "Good night . . . good-bye," he declared to the adoring crowd in San Francisco, California, at the Winterland Ballroom.

Here is the story of how it all started.

Sleeping, 1945

"Sweet dreams, hon." Jaime's mom clicked the dial on the radio above his crib as a boogie-woogie groove seeped out of the small tweed speaker. Jaime lay still, eyes wide, with an unusual level of patience and wonderment for a two-year-old.

We Are the People of the Longhouse

Jaime Royal Robertson was born in Toronto, Ontario, in Canada, an only child of a Mohawk Indian mother and a Jewish professional gambler. His family lived in a small apartment that they shared with relatives. When he was a little older, kids from the neighborhood started calling him Robbie because of his last name, and the nickname stuck.

Summers, holidays, and many weekends were spent at the Six Nations Indian Reservation where Robbie's mother had been born and raised. Robbie and his mom would take a two-hour bus ride from Toronto up to the reservation. It was here that it all began; it was here where the rhythm, melodies, and storytelling of Robbie's First Nation relatives captured his imagination.

Days were spent picking wild strawberries, fishing for rainbow trout in the Grand River, and swimming in the rock quarry. At night when they gathered around a fire pit where flames reached upward and licked the crisp night air, the storytelling began. An elder chief would tell vivid tales of talking coyote and ravens who stole the sun.

As the bus pulled off the dirt road of the reservation to the pavement of the highway back to Toronto, Robbie would stare out the window, waving good-bye. "Hey, Ma, I wanna be the storyteller one day."

Whenever Robbie's First Nation relatives visited him in the city, they were always sure to bring along guitars, mandolins, and maybe even a drum or two. His uncle taught him a few chords, and Robbie locked his sights on guitar. That year on Christmas morning, Robbie rushed to the tree and found a shiny, dark-wood acoustic guitar with a painting of a cowboy on it. He strummed his first chords on his own guitar.

Lessons were the next order of business. "Your hands are too small to play that Spanish-style guitar," said Billy Blue, Robbie's first guitar teacher. "We're gonna have to start you off on Hawaiian, son."

Only a few months into his guitar lessons, Robbie decided to take things into his own hands. He applied what he learned and set out to teach himself the rest.

As soon as Robbie finished his homework, he would play guitar for hours. When his parents had gone to sleep, he would quietly click on the small transistor radio and listen to his musical heroes being broadcast by a deejay named The Hound, out of Buffalo, New York.

Elvis Presley

Little Richard

Chuck Berry

Somewhere Down the Crazy River

On the reservation, eleven-year-old Robbie had surpassed the adults as the best guitarist. "You're getting really good." "That kid can play." "Look at that guitar boogie." It was these words of encouragement that kept Robbie inspired.

By the time Robbie was twelve, music consumed him. Little Richard, Gene Vincent and The Blue Caps, Carl Perkins, Buddy Holly, Elvis Presley, Chuck Berry, and Jimmy Reed were Robbie's heroes. He'd hear their songs on the radio and play them on guitar, and before long, he was making up songs of his own.

At thirteen, Robbie teamed up with a few kids in the neighborhood and formed his first band—Robbie Robertson and the Rhythm Chords.

Stage Fright—"We're the Opening Act!"

Robbie and the Rhythm Chords played some shows around town and before long got their big break. They were scheduled to open for a popular group called Ronnie Hawkins and The Hawks. All the kids from high school would be coming down to the arena to see the two bands perform.

Robbie's unique guitar playing immediately caught the attention of Ronnie Hawkins. Ronnie invited Robbie to hang out with him and his band. Seizing the opportunity, Robbie did whatever he could to make himself useful. He would get the guys sodas, string a guitar, or pick up lunch. One day he overheard Ronnie having a conversation with his agent. "I'm gonna need some songs for my new record."

Robbie raced home, locked himself in his room, and started writing songs in hopes of impressing Ronnie. "Dinner time, hon," Robbie's mom called. "No time to eat, Ma. I'm on a mission."

A couple of days later, Robbie met with Ronnie Hawkins and played him the two songs he'd written—"Hey Boba Lu" and "Someone Like You." Both songs would appear on Ronnie's next album, *Mr. Dynamo*. Robbie, now sixteen, had begun to make his mark.

The next step was going to New York City and the famous Brill Building. The Brill Building was where the greatest rock and roll songwriters worked. Robbie met with Leiber and Stoller, who wrote "Hound Dog" and "Jailhouse Rock," Pomus and Shuman, who wrote "This Magic Moment," and Otis Blackwell, who wrote "Great Balls of Fire." His musical education was now in session.

Endless Highway—
"Hey, Robbie! Ready to Take a Shot?"

An invitation arrived to try out to be the full-time guitarist for The Hawks. After a solemn promise to finish school when he returned and an agreement to send money home, his mom decided to let him go. But how to get there? Unable to afford a ticket, Robbie did the unspeakable: he sold his Fender Stratocaster guitar and amplifier—a gift from his mother—to pay for the ticket. And he didn't even have the gig yet! But what he did have was the drive and belief that there was something special out there waiting for him.

With no guitar and just a small suitcase of clothes, Robbie hopped the train headed for the Ozark Mountains in Fayetteville, Arkansas, a long way from home. The first stop was St. Louis, Missouri, where Robbie would switch to a bus to complete his journey.

Canadian Cold Front Moving In

It was January and still freezing in Canada, but when Robbie arrived in Arkansas, the sun was out. Ronnie and The Hawks were there to greet him. "We gotta get you some new clothes, son. I can't be seen with you dressed like that," Ronnie said as the boys laughed at Robbie's Canadian reversible winter overcoat.

After a quick stop where Ronnie bought some corduroy pants and a shirt for Robbie, they piled into a long Cadillac with a trailer attached to the back. A large hawk was painted on the trailer, and folks waved to the boys in the band as they drove through town headed for Helena, Arkansas, to start rehearsing.

A snag in the plan! The lead guitarist of The Hawks decided to stay on a little longer but the bass guitar player was leaving the band immediately. Robbie stepped up and learned all the songs on bass guitar but in his room at night he taught himself the guitar parts too, waiting and preparing for his moment to become the lead guitarist of The Hawks.

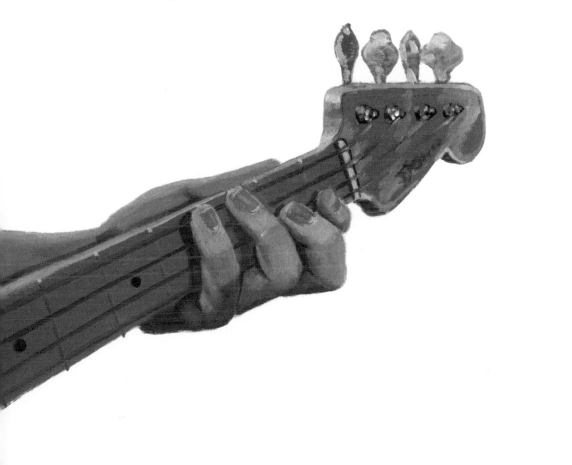

One afternoon, Robbie went to nearby Memphis, Tennessee, and visited Home of the Blues, a record shop on Beale Street. He had received fifty dollars for his tryout for The Hawks and spent the entire amount on records by Howlin' Wolf, Muddy Waters, BB King, and other blues legends. He also stopped into Sun Records and had the good fortune to watch legendary rock-and-roller Jerry Lee Lewis in the studio making a record.

The fire burned inside Robbie even hotter now. Back at the motel after seeing Jerry Lee Lewis in action, and with a stack of new records to listen to and learn to play, Robbie practiced obsessively. That special thing he believed was out there for him was now in reach. Robbie played until he couldn't feel his fingers. He even slept with his guitar.

After hearing how well Robbie had learned The Hawks' set list, Ronnie Hawkins was very pleased. "You've got the job . . . *for now* . . . as the bassist. So let's go play some shows!" Robbie hadn't seen his mom in a few months and couldn't wait to get to Canada. When they reached Toronto, Robbie's mom sat in the front row and cheered her son on. While on tour, The Hawks' guitarist, Fred Carter Jr., finally bid farewell to the band to pursue a steadier lifestyle as a studio musician.

Tryouts began for the guitarist position, and Robbie got the job! Ronnie and The Hawks would play five 30-minute sets a day, and after the shows, Robbie would head to his room to practice. This caught Ronnie Hawkins's attention.

The Axman's Coming

Not many players were bending guitar strings at the time. By pressing down on the string and bending it upward, a player could stretch the pitch of the note by a half step or two. Robbie took the influence from the blues records he bought and began bending the strings while creating a feverish vibrato. At a gig in Toronto, Buddy Holly told Robbie that in order to create a fuzzier, more distorted sound, he would make a slit with a razor blade in the speaker of his amp. Robbie quickly applied the razor blade trick, cranked his amp full blast, and played a Fender Telecaster, creating a unique, screaming guitar tone. It was now 1961 and people came from far and wide to hear the hottest, youngest guitar player around.

By 1964, The Hawks' lineup was Robbie on guitar, Richard Manuel on piano, Rick Danko on bass guitar, Garth Hudson on organ and sax, Levon Helm on drums, and Ronnie Hawkins on lead vocals.

After a few more years with Ronnie, these five talented musicians went out on their own. Leaving their mentor Ronnie Hawkins wasn't an easy decision but the time had come.

Following some gigs through the South, The Hawks, now with drummer Levon Helm on lead vocals, ended up in Somers Point, New Jersey, to play a club. At the hotel before the show, a very interesting phone call came in. A famous folksinger by the name of Bob Dylan asked Robbie if he could come to New York City to meet with him. The folksinger scene wasn't something that The Hawks had come in contact with, so Robbie, not really knowing who Bob Dylan was, decided that it couldn't hurt to go see what this guy was up to.

Robbie and Bob Dylan sat down with guitars, sang songs, and talked about music. Bob Dylan offered Robbie a gig on the spot. Robbie was intrigued by Bob's music and wanted to be a part of it. Robbie told Bob that he really needed to meet the rest of The Hawks.

Going Electric

In 1965, Bob Dylan and The Hawks headed out on a tour
through North America, Europe, Australia, and the United
Kingdom. Little did anyone know that this tour would change
the face of rock and roll.

At the time, Bob Dylan was a successful folk artist who
mainly performed alone with an acoustic guitar. So when he
was accompanied by an electric rock and roll band, his fans felt
betrayed. Fans turned up in droves, selling out every show, but
they weren't cheering him on—rather they booed in protest.
Robbie became skilled at playing his guitar
without looking at his fingers in order
to avoid the flying objects flung
from the angry audiences.

Even with the negative reaction, Bob Dylan and The Hawks
felt they were on the cusp of something groundbreaking. In fact,
it was a musical revolution, and they were smack-dab in the middle
of it. Rock and roll music, and especially lyrical content, was taking
a new turn. No more "Baby, baby, I love you" lyrics. This was an
introspective style that reached music fans on a whole new level.

Andy Warhol *Marilyn Monroe* *Salvador Dalí*

Robbie moved into the Chelsea Hotel in New York City after the tour. Andy Warhol, Marilyn Monroe, and Salvador Dalí were all a part of the scene.

At this point, The Hawks were preparing for another tour, but Bob Dylan was injured in a motorcycle accident and couldn't go on the road. Robbie and his bandmates headed upstate to Bob Dylan's house in Woodstock, New York, to write and record some songs.

Music from Big Pink

Woodstock, New York, was an art colony with a small-town attitude, and this pleased the boys just fine. They adapted to a communal vibe wherein one guy would make the coffee, one would fix a creaky screen door, and one would cook breakfast. All the while, they were developing their music in the basement of a house that was known as Big Pink. When they would go into town for some supplies, the merchants all referred to them as "the band." Bob Dylan also would simply refer to them as "the band." The name stuck and The Band was born.

Early one morning, Robbie was sitting with his pencil, paper, and his Martin D28 acoustic guitar across his lap. It was time to really begin the writing process for their first album. *If I can just get the first line of the song down*, he thought to himself. Waiting for inspiration, Robbie peered into the sound hole of the guitar. It read, "Nazareth." Quickly he picked up the pencil and wrote the line "I pulled into Nazareth." In a few hours he had written one of The Band's most famous songs—"The Weight." The lyrics spoke of Anna Lee, Crazy Chester, Jack the Dog, and Luke My Friend, all characters Robbie had encountered on the road with The Hawks.

When *Music from Big Pink* was released it was unlike any music heard before. Its roots were deeply embedded in the American landscape but the delivery was entirely unique—a mix of mountain music, Delta blues, rhythm and blues, Canadian folk, and rockabilly. There wasn't a name for it then, but there is now. It's called Americana Music, and The Band was instrumental in its creation.

Not only did The Band create a timeless sound, they also had a look that was original. It was as if they stumbled out of the 1800s right on to the psychedelic rock scene of the 1960s.

Across the Great Divide

Tired of digging themselves out of the snow, Robbie and the guys moved to sunny Los Angeles, California, for their second record. They rented the entertainer Sammy Davis Jr.'s house in the Hollywood Hills and brought with them that same clubhouse, down-home sensibility. The Band converted the pool house into a full-blown recording studio. During this time, Robbie wrote more songs that further defined the genre of music they had created. "King Harvest (Has Surely Come)" told of hard times for farmers and spoke proudly of union workers and their system. He also penned "The Night They Drove Old Dixie Down," a vivid portrait of the Civil War told from the standpoint of a fictional character from the South named Virgil Caine.

The Band had created such a stir musically that in 1970 they were the first North American band and only the second band in history behind The Beatles to be featured on the cover of *Time* Magazine. The article heralded them as "The first to match the excellence of The Beatles."

On July 28, 1973, Robbie prepared to take the stage. The Band was playing a one-day event with The Grateful Dead and The Allman Brothers at Watkins Glen raceway in upstate New York. He walked onto the stage and looked into the massive crowd of over 650,000 people. With a quick nod to the audience, Robbie cranked up his guitar and The Band kicked into "Goin' Back to Memphis," a Chuck Berry song that he learned sitting at the foot of his bed many years ago. Robbie had traveled far from his roots in Canada on the Indian reservation to playing with Ronnie Hawkins and Bob Dylan and now here. An epic journey on the rock and roll highway.

Timeline

1943: Jaime Royal Robertson is born on July 5 in Toronto, Ontario. After kids and teachers shorten his last name to Robbie, the nickname Robbie sticks. Robbie is an only child. His mother, Rose Marie Chrysler, is a full-blooded Indian from the Six Nations, Mohawk Tribe.

Robbie, age two, circa 1945

1956: Forms his first band with older kids from the neighborhood—Robbie Robertson and The Rhythm Chords.

Robbie and his mom, circa 1945

1959: Leaves high school early to join Ronnie Hawkins and The Hawks as guitarist.

1960–65: Goes on tour with Ronnie Hawkins, playing the famous Chitlin Circuit in the Deep South of America and all over Canada.

1965: Meets and becomes the lead guitarist for Bob Dylan. They do some recording on Dylan's album *Blonde on Blonde*, and they go on a historic tour of the world.

1967: The Hawks change their name to The Band and record the album *The Basement Tapes* with Bob Dylan. Robbie marries Dominique Bourgeois.

1968: Robbie's first daughter, Alexandra, is born.

1968–69: The Band releases groundbreaking albums *Music from Big Pink* and a self-titled release. The Beatles and Eric Clapton become instant admirers.

1970: The Band is the first North American group to be featured on the cover of *Time* Magazine. Robbie's second daughter, Delphine, is born.

Robbie, circa 1946

1972: The Band performs with The Grateful Dead and The Allman Brothers at Watkins Glen raceway for an audience of 650,000 people. The *Guinness Book of World Records* declares the attendance the largest in rock and roll history.

1970–73: The Band releases four more albums: *Stage Fright, Cahoots, Moondog Matinee,* and a live album *Rock of Ages.*

Robbie Robertson and The Rhythm Chords, circa 1957

1974: Bob Dylan and The Band reunite to record an album called *Planet Waves* and go on one of the most successful world tours of the time. Robbie's son, Sebastian, is born.

1975: The Band releases a sixth studio album, *Northern Lights, Southern Cross*. The album the group recorded nearly ten years earlier with Bob Dylan, *The Basement Tapes*, is also released.

1976: The Band's final concert is filmed by Martin Scorsese and called *The Last Waltz*.

1977: The final album by The Band is released, entitled *Islands*.

1980–86: Robbie turns his focus to creating music for films like *Raging Bull*, *The King of Comedy*, and *The Color of Money*.

The Hawks, circa 1963: Rick Danko, Richard Manuel, Levon Helm, Garth Hudson, and Robbie Robertson

1987: Robbie releases his first solo album with featured guests U2 and Peter Gabriel. The album wins the Juno Award for Album of the Year, and Robbie wins for Producer of the Year.

1989: The Band is inducted into the Canadian Music Hall of Fame.

1991: Robbie travels to New Orleans to record his second solo album, *Storyville*.

1994: The Band is inducted into the Rock and Roll Hall of Fame. Robbie returns to his roots, releasing his third solo album called *Music for the Native Americans*.

Robbie and Sebastian, circa 1976

1997: Robbie receives the lifetime achievement award from the National Academy of Songwriters.

1999: Robbie writes and records *Contact from the Underworld of Redboy*, another album of musical exploration into his Native North American roots.

2002: Robbie continues his musical work with Martin Scorsese on *Gangs of New York*.

2003: After delivering an address to the graduating class of Queen's University in Kingston, Ontario, Robbie is awarded an honorary doctorate. He also receives a star on Canada's Walk of Fame.

2008: The Band is given a Grammy Lifetime Achievement Award.

2011: Robbie releases his fifth solo album, *How to Become Clairvoyant*, which has his highest opening week at number 13 on the *Billboard* charts. He is inducted into the Canadian Songwriters Hall of Fame, receives the Royal Order of Canada, and is honored with his face on a Canadian postage stamp.

Robbie Robertson stamp (part of the Canadian Recording Artists series)

Sebastian Robertson and Robbie Robertson

An Interview with My Dad, Robbie Robertson

The most important thing that I took from writing this book and what I urge all readers to do is a simple and priceless project: INTERVIEW YOUR PARENTS! What follows is a Q&A with my father—a father, who has shown me the way with the utmost in love, care, and understanding. I encourage you to make a list of questions for your own parents and record your conversation so you can capture that history.

Sebastian Robertson: Were you surprised that your mom let you go on the road with Ronnie Hawkins at such a young age?

Robbie Robertson: It didn't happen suddenly, so I wasn't surprised. It took a lot of doing to convince my mother that if I didn't go I could regret it for the rest of my life. And God knows now (LAUGHS) I *would* have regretted it for the rest of my life. But my mother made a deal with me. She very much admired Ronnie Hawkins and knew him before I did because she was old enough to go into those clubs. Everyone wanted to see Ronnie Hawkins

Robbie, age 17, circa 1960

and The Hawks when they came to Toronto, and she had met Ron. Years later, Ronnie told me that my mom would tell him, "One day, you're going to meet my son, and he's a very talented boy and probably he's going to be working with you." My mother said if I could get a job playing with Ronnie Hawkins and really make a living and take care of myself, then we had a deal, but anything less than that and I would have to go back to school.

SR: After you went on the road, were you able to keep up your friendships with the kids back home?

RR: Quite a few of my friends were music people. For instance, Pete Traynor invented Traynor Amplifiers in Canada, which was *the* amp in Canada just like Vox is *the* amp in England. I would see some of the musicians I used to play with when I would come back to Canada because they were curious about what was going on with The Hawks. Other friends I didn't feel as connected to anymore because my interest went in a very specific direction. The people I did keep in touch with were all involved in music; basically, if they had a connection to music, that carried us on.

A postcard from Robbie to his mom, 1960

SR: Do you get nervous when you play live?

RR: This is a two-part answer for me. In the really early days I never thought about it. I was just so excited about playing. Also when I played with Bob Dylan it didn't cross my mind. Then, some years later with The Band, we recorded our first record, *Music from Big Pink*. Soon after, Rick Danko was in a bad car accident and was in the hospital in traction. He had broken his neck, and we didn't play for a while. When it was time to play again, we were invited to perform at the Woodstock festival for 500,000 people and that was a bit overwhelming. We were starting out on such a high scale that we couldn't help but feel kind of nervous. After tirelessly working on an album, and with my baby daughter at home, we had to go and play a show in San Francisco at the Winterland Ballroom, and I got really sick. Our manager called in a hypnotist to try and help get me out on the stage. It suddenly dawned on me—how much of this was my being rundown mentally and physically and how much of this was stage fright?

SR: You wrote a song called "Stage Fright." Is that song about you?

RR: That song is about being aware of what stage fright is. I didn't write songs strictly about me. I wrote songs about characters and stories. I didn't feel comfortable writing about myself.

SR: Coming from Canada, were there any particular foods or drinks that you found especially delicious when you arrived in the American South?

RR: Levon Helm took me to his parents' house, and his mother cooked a quintessential Southern meal and with that meal you had to have an RC Cola. Levon told me it just didn't go down right if you don't have an RC. I had never had an RC. I thought everything was the real thing down there. This is where rock and roll was born. I thought everything was better in the South. And barbeque pork— barbeque in the Delta was shredded pork. They cooked it in a pit in the ground for a hundred hours (LAUGHS) until it melted in your mouth. They put the shredded pork and a special sauce on a burger bun, and it was like nothing I'd ever eaten before. It was out of this world.

SR: What was your regimen for practicing guitar?

RR: When I first joined Ronnie Hawkins's band, my regimen was twenty-four hours a day because I had to prove myself. I slept with a guitar or a bass. And if I woke up in the night, I picked it up and played. I practiced all day and all night and played gigs in between. Ronnie Hawkins said he'd never seen anyone sleep with a guitar before.

SR: How did you learn to play other instruments, like the piano?

RR: There were always very interesting piano players among Ronnie Hawkins and The Hawks, and because I was standing next to them on stage, I was intrigued by what they could do. I would get the piano players to show me some of their tricks. But what the piano really became for me was an instrument to compose on. It would make me do different things than what I'd do on guitar. I'd say about half my songs were written on the piano.

SR: Besides music, did you have any other hobbies to occupy your time when you were on the road?

RR: My main hobby on the road was reading. I became infatuated with Southern writers.

The Band: Rick Danko, Levon Helm, Robbie Robertson, Richard Manuel, and Garth Hudson

SR: What were some of your favorite books?

RR: I was reading classics by [John] Steinbeck, [William] Faulkner, and [Ernest] Hemingway. Because I was missing out on school, reading became a necessity—some kind of instinctual draw that I had to have.

SR: What are some of the ways in which you come up with song ideas?

RR: Song ideas for the most part come from a fluke of imagination. I wish there was a deeper explanation. However, some of the songs I wrote were about historical times and events, and the reading I was doing really helped me paint pictures with the lyrics and expand my vocabulary. Gotta read to write.

For Donovan
—S. R.

For the Beefalo Brothers
—A. G.

Robbie Robertson, age 4

Henry Holt and Company, LLC
Publishers since 1866
175 Fifth Avenue
New York, New York 10010
mackids.com

Henry Holt® is a registered trademark of Henry Holt and Company, LLC.
Text copyright © 2014 by Sebastian Robertson
Illustrations copyright © 2014 by Adam Gustavson
All rights reserved.

Library of Congress Cataloging-in-Publication Data is available.

ISBN 978-0-8050-9473-2

Henry Holt books may be purchased for business or promotional use. For information
on bulk purchases, please contact Macmillan Corporate and Premium Sales Department
at (800) 221-7945 x5442 or by e-mail at specialmarkets@macmillan.com.

First Edition—2014 / Designed by Patrick Collins
The artist used oil paint on prepared paper to create the illustrations for this book.
Printed in China by Toppan Leefung Printing Ltd., Dongguan City, Guangdong Province

1 3 5 7 9 10 8 6 4 2